The Triumph of Mystery

"Casting down imaginations, and every high thing that exalteth itself against the knowledge of God, and bringing into captivity every thought to the obedience of Christ" (2 Corinthians 10:5).

The Triumph of Mystery

Theology and Science at the Intersection of Humility and Wonder

DJK Institute Essays
Book 1

Dr. Michael A. Milton

In Memory of

The Rev. Dr. and Mrs. Robert L. Reymond, Sr.

"Beloved, we are God's children now, and what we will be has not yet appeared; but we know that when he appears we shall be like him, because we shall see him as he is."

— The Apostle John (1 John 3:2)

Contents

About the Institute

The D. James Kennedy Institute
Essays Series

The D. James Kennedy Institute Essays series is dedicated to exploring and articulating the profound truths of the Christian faith through faithful biblical exegesis and pastoral application. Our burden is to ensure that every reader, particularly pastors and seminarians, is equipped with a deep understanding of Scripture, enabling them to teach and apply the Bible's timeless truths effectively in their ministries.

Inspired by a Kuyperian vision, this series seeks to apply the Gospel and the Lordship of Christ to all areas of life. We believe that every sphere of human existence, whether personal, social, or cultural, falls under the sovereign rule of Jesus Christ. Each essay in this series endeavors to integrate theological insights with practical applications, encouraging believers to live out their faith in every aspect of their lives.

Through rigorous scholarship and heartfelt pastoral concern, the D. James Kennedy Institute Essays aim to bridge the gap between academic theology and real-world ministry. By doing so, we hope to cultivate a generation of Christian leaders who are not only well-versed in doctrinal truths but also adept at applying these truths to the challenges and opportunities they face in their congregations and communities.

Join us on this journey of discovery and application as we seek to glorify God by proclaiming His Word and demonstrating His Lordship in all things.

MICHAEL A. MILTON
First Sunday after Pentecost 2024

Chapter 1

How Shall We Then Reason?

First Things

"If the believer's God is at work in this world, then in this world the believer's hand must take hold of the plow, and the name of the Lord must be glorified in that activity as well."[1]

— Abraham Kuyper (1837-1920)

How shall we then reason? This is my question as we study scientific data from a materialistic view and quickly arrive at the logical extremity of the argu-

---

1. Abraham Kuyper, *Common Grace: God's Gifts for a Fallen World, Volume 1* (Bellevue, WA: Lexham Press, 2016), 23.

refusing to engage with theology.[2] Dr. David Gelernter (1945–) once remarked in the *Claremont Review of Books*,

> "Darwinism is no longer just a scientific theory but the basis of a worldview, and an emergency religion for many troubled souls who need one."[3]

Gelernter, a renowned mathematical scholar, was responding to Stephen Meyer's *Darwin's Doubt* and expanded his thoughts on an episode of "Mathematical Challenges to Darwin's Theory of Evolution" at Stanford University's Hoover Institution.[4,5] He added, "The world is a mess."[6] When Meyer responded by saying that theology affirms what we observe in the material world, namely, that there is both intelligent design and the presence of entropy, he was pointing to a profound truth. This fits perfectly with the Judeo-Christian concept of the fall of man, which introduced sin into the world.[7] We see this in the unchecked multiplication of mutations, creating extraordinarily dangerous bacteria and other disease-carrying entities. Dr. Gelernter not only conceded Meyer's argument

---

2. I am indebted to the outstanding scholarship in David Snoke, "The Apologetic Argument," *The American Scientific Affiliation* 50, no. June (1998): 108–21, https://www.asa3.org/ASA/PSCF/1998/PSCF6-98dyn.html. The title of this paper is a play on words from the essential book on practical apologetics, Francis A. Schaeffer, *How Should We Then Live? (L'Abri 50th Anniversary Edition): The Rise and Decline of Western Thought and Culture* (Wheaton, IL: Crossway, 2005).

3. David Gelernter, "Giving Up Darwin: A Fond Farewell to a Brilliant and Beautiful Theory," *Claremont Review of Books* 19, no. 2 (Spring 2019).

4. Stephen C. Meyer, *Darwin's Doubt: The Explosive Origin of Animal Life and the Case for Intelligent Design* (San Francisco: Harper Collins, 2013).

5. *Mathematical Challenges to Darwin's Theory of Evolution*, 2019, https://www.youtube.com/watch?v=noj4phMT9OE.

6. Dr. David Gelenter on *Mathematical Challenges*.

7. *On the Fall of Man, see* Joel R. Beeke and Sinclair B. Ferguson, *Reformed Confessions Harmonized* (Baker Publishing Group, 1999), 46, 47, 49.

but added that theology must be included in scientific inquiry because science arrives at dead ends in almost every area of inquiry. The only bridge to the logical progression of thought is built by theology.

Questions for Reflection

1. How does my worldview influence my interpretation of scientific data?

• Reflect on how your beliefs shape your understanding of scientific discoveries and theories. Consider how this worldview aligns or conflicts with materialistic perspectives.

2. IN WHAT WAYS CAN THEOLOGY AND SCIENCE complement each other in my understanding of the world?

• Contemplate the potential harmony between theological truths and scientific facts. Think about how integrating both can provide a more comprehensive view of reality.

3. HOW DO I RESPOND TO THE IDEA THAT DARWINISM CAN function as an "emergency religion" for some?

• Consider why Darwinism might serve as a substitute religion for certain individuals. Reflect on the implications of this for both personal faith and wider cultural engagement.

4. WHAT ROLE DOES THE CONCEPT OF ENTROPY PLAY IN MY understanding of creation and the fall of man?

• Reflect on how the scientific principle of entropy aligns with the theological concept of the fall. Consider how this understanding impacts your view of the natural world and human history.

. . .

5. How can I effectively engage in discussions about intelligent design and evolution with those who hold different views?

• Think about strategies for respectful and meaningful dialogue. Reflect on how to present your beliefs in a way that invites open and constructive conversation.

6. In what ways can my Christian faith inform my approach to scientific inquiries and challenges?

• Consider how your theological convictions can guide your scientific pursuits and responses to scientific challenges. Reflect on how faith can provide insight and direction in areas where science reaches its limits.

Chapter 2

The Interplay of Science and Theology

More than you Think

"Of course, I reject atheism because I believe Christianity to be true. But I also reject it because I am a **scientist**. How could I be impressed with a worldview that undermines the very rationality we need to do science? Science and God mix very well. It is science and atheism that do not mix."[1]

— John Lennox (b. 1943)

As you might guess, I completely agree. Dr. Gelernter's concern that science, as the adopted closed-minded and biased worldview, limits or even excludes the necessity of theological dialogue is unquestionably true. For instance, when fossils of whales were found in Chile's Atacama Desert, elevated far above sea level, materialistic,

---

1. Quoted in William A. Dembski, Casey Luskin, and Joseph M. Holden, *The Comprehensive Guide to Science and Faith: Exploring the Ultimate Questions About Life and the Cosmos* (Eugene, OR: Harvest House Publishers, 2021), 130.

unbelieving scientists went to remarkable extremes to invent theories to support the discovery (e.g., the whales ate deadly algae, the shoreline built up over millions of years, and the remains somehow survived decay and carcass-scavengers as they became covered by sand).[2] However, *Occam's Razor*—the simplest explanation is usually the correct one—guides us to see that a catastrophic flood brought these creatures inland to the elevated desert-like conditions and then compressed them with the right amount of water pressure, debris, and temperature, preventing ordinary decay or consumption by scavengers.[3] Mercifully, there are scientists who are unafraid to ditch the materialistic worldview and to inquire without that bias.[4]

The flood story, the story of Noah, and a remnant of life on an ark are anthropological common denominators in the human story.[5] Scripture, proven time and again to be a historically accurate ancient record, explains the catastrophic flood in context. Remarkably, biased scientists must reject archaeology, ancient literature, history, and common sense to protect their materialistic view. The same is true with the age of the Earth. The same is true with the soft tissue remains of dinosaurs.[6]

---

2. See, e.g., "Chile's Stunning Fossil Whale Graveyard Explained," *BBC News*, February 26, 2014, sec. Science & Environment, https://www.bbc.com/news/science-environment-26343894.

3. On Occam's Razor and William of Occam's (1285–1349) theological authority for his observations, see, e.g., Eric W. Hagedorn, "The Changing Role of Theological Authority in Ockham's Razor," *Res Philosophica* 99, no. 2 (2022): 97–120, https://doi.org/10.11612/resphil.2165.

4. See, e.g., *Whale Fossils in the Desert - Evidence for a Worldwide Flood?*, 2023, https://www.youtube.com/watch?v=QUV8dEIQYt8.

5. See, e.g., *Whale Fossils in the Desert - Evidence for a Worldwide Flood?*, 2023, https://www.youtube.com/watch?v=QUV8dEIQYt8. See, also, Louis H. Feldman, "Josephus' Portrait of Noah and Its Parallels in Philo, Pseudo-Philo's 'Biblical Antiquities', and Rabbinic Midrashim," *Proceedings of the American Academy for Jewish Research* 55 (1988): 31–57, https://doi.org/10.2307/3622676.

6. See, e.g., Michael J. Oard. "The Extinction of the Dinosaurs." *Journal of*

Worldview is a powerful variable that is (that must be) preeminent in *the order of calculations.*[7] To observe without the lens of truth, i.e., lacking even an *a priori* sense of a cosmos and a Creator, is to arrive at the wrong answer. The Dutch professor Herman Bavinck (1854-1921), one of the most erudite and insightful theologians and philosophers in the West, reflected on the fundamental crisis of *Modernism* in his day:

> "Bavinck began his book *Christelijke Wereldbeschouwing,* or *Christian Worldview,* by noting the consequence of this 'modern' problem: 'Before all else, what strikes us in the modern age is the internal discord that consumes the self.'"[8]

The gifted Dr. Bavinck added a helpful reflection,

> "What is the relation between thinking and being, between being and becoming, and between becoming and acting? What am I? What is the world, and what is my place and task within this world? Autonomous thinking finds no satisfactory answer to these questions and oscillates between materialism and spiritualism, between atomism and dynamism, between nomism and antinomianism. But Christianity preserves the harmony [between them] and reveals to us a wisdom

---

Creation 11, no. 2 (1997): 137-154. Valuable insights on the cosmological arguments and Holy Scripture may be found in Jonathan D. Safarti. D. Russell Humphreys' "Cosmology and the Timothy Test: A Reply." *Creation Ex Nihilo Technical Journal,* 11, no. 2 (1997): 195-198.

7. That is, as in mathematics, the "order of operations:" or, PEMDAS.

8. Herman Bavinck, *Christian Worldview* (Wheaton: Crossway, 2019), "Introduction," in the digital version.

that reconciles the human being with God and, through this, with itself, with the world, and with life."[9]

Thus, science must recognize the value of metaphysics in the order of operations as surely as theology must recognize matter. To do otherwise is to scramble the equation and guarantee distortion. As we all know, distortion of reality is a serious existential situation that leads to delusion, and delusion leads to death.

9. Herman Bavinck, *Christelijke Wereldbeschouwing* (Kampen: J. H. Kok, 1929), 14.

"De problemen, waarvoor de menschelijke geest altijd weer te staan komt, zijn deze: wat is de verhouding van denken en zijn, van zijn en worden, van worden en handelen? Wat ben ik, wat is de wereld en wat is in die wereldmine plaats en mijn taak?"

Questions for Reflection

1. How does my worldview influence my interpretation of scientific discoveries and biblical narratives?

• Reflect on how your beliefs shape your understanding of scientific and theological explanations. Consider how this worldview aligns or conflicts with materialistic perspectives.

2. What are the implications of excluding theological dialogue from scientific inquiry?

• Contemplate the consequences of ignoring theological insights in scientific discussions. Reflect on how this exclusion might limit our understanding of both the natural world and spiritual truths.

3. How can Occam's Razor be applied to reconcile scientific evidence with biblical accounts, such as the flood narrative?

• Reflect on how the principle of Occam's Razor can help find the simplest explanations that align with both scientific evidence and biblical stories. Consider the balance between simplicity and thoroughness.

4. In what ways do my theological beliefs shape my approach to understanding the age of the Earth and the existence of soft tissue remains in dinosaurs?

• Think about how your faith informs your views on these scientific topics. Reflect on how this perspective might differ from a purely materialistic view and what evidence supports your stance.

5. How can Bavinck's reflections on the crisis of Modernism and the role of Christianity in preserving harmony between thinking, being, and acting influence my view of science and theology?

• Reflect on Bavinck's insights and consider how they apply to the current interplay between scientific and theological perspectives. Think about the importance of a Christian worldview in resolving these fundamental questions.

6. What steps can I take to integrate metaphysical considerations into my scientific explorations while also acknowledging the physical realities addressed by theology?

• Consider practical ways to incorporate metaphysical questions into scientific studies. Reflect on how acknowledging both the physical and metaphysical aspects can lead to a more holistic understanding of truth.

~

Chapter 3

Embracing Mystery in Theology and Science

The Strength of Limitations

"So where I cannot find bottom in the depths, I must take account of human weakness, not condemn divine authority. I certainly exclaim, and I'm not in the least ashamed of it, Oh, the depths of the riches of the wisdom and knowledge of God! How inscrutable are his judgments and untraceable his ways! For my part, I fortify my weakness with these words."

— Augustine of Hippo (354-430 AD)

One of the things you will often hear from aging theologians and pastors like myself is this: "I give more room for mystery these days." This humility is cultivated after years of questions and observations and through a deep study of the Word of God. It is a virtue that induces doxology:

"Oh, the depth of the riches and wisdom and knowledge of God! How inscrutable are his judgments and how unsearchable his ways" (Romans 11:33)!

How is Mystery a Virtue?

We should be clear about mystery (if that appears oxymoronic, then we have succeeded in affirming two truths that are in tension). We do not mean to propose "mystery" in place of rigorous scholarship, nor do we imply that mystery is an elusive force that evades logic. On the contrary, mystery is logical. It is a known, unknowable variable in scientific or theological equations.

In the matter of soteriology—how one is forgiven and redeemed—Almighty God is altogether sovereign. Jesus said, "The wind blows where it wills" (John 3:8). Yet, we are culpable for our unbelief. There is mystery in this variable. God has revealed much but not all. We live in the tension of this mystery, or we invent answers for the unknowable. The former response requires reasonable faith in a God who has revealed Truth. The former proceeds on speculation.

In science, electricity is both a wave and a particle. These seemingly contradictory properties coexist, creating a mystery. Perhaps someone will provide an answer by the time of this writing. Some mysteries are only temporary, as science is always on a journey of discovery. Theology, however, is on an adventure of classifying dogmatics to make sense of the world. General revelations—God's handprint on the cosmos—and Special Revelation—the Word of God written and incarnate through our Lord Jesus Christ—become a starting point for observation and adventure. Thus, we have those like Isaac Newton (1643-1727) or Michael Faraday (1791-1867), believing scientists who started with God's revelation. For example, Michael Faraday's Christian faith led to some of the most helpful inventions we enjoy. And his discoveries began from a worldview that would influence the world forever:

> Faraday was committed to *seeking truth*. A particular Christian emphasis in his thinking was his view of the natural world as something created and governed by a God who had given rules that human beings could and should follow. Inspired by a vision that everything in nature was ultimately connected, he peered forward into the future, anticipating ideas that were to be developed by Einstein, who had a portrait of Faraday in his office to inspire him.[1]

We not only affirm God's wisdom, strength, grace, and mercy in observing the world around us. We admit our weaknesses. Recognizing one's limitations is both honorable and economical. In this sense, mystery—admitting the unknowable—is a virtue.

Mystery can be a cop-out, but if we have studied the Word of God, taken what is revealed, and restrained from speculation, we end up with mystery. Deuteronomy 29:29 says,

> "The secret things belong to the Lord our God, but the things revealed belong to us and to our children forever."

The admission of theological limitations due to divine concealment is a necessary posture for accurate exegesis. Thus,

---

1. J. John, "Lessons in Faith from Michael Faraday, the Brilliant Christian Scientist Who Rose from Poverty and Obscurity," *Christian Today*, February 26, 2021, https://www.christiantoday.com/article/lessons.in.faith.from. michael.faraday.the.brilliant.christian.scientist.who.rose.from.poverty.and. obscurity/136432.htm.

even the great Augustine of Hippo, perhaps the greatest theologian since Paul, demonstrated an easy appreciation for mystery in his study for preaching and teaching. Of the doctrine of election taught by Paul in Romans chapter 9, Augustine writes:

> "Are you expecting me to tell you why he has mercy on whom he will, and whose will he hardens? Are you expecting it from me, a man? If you're a human being and I'm a human being, then both of us have heard: *who are you to answer back to God* (Rom 9:20)? So trusting ignorance is better than rash knowledge. God says to me, Christ speaks through the apostle, O man, who are you to answer back to God? And I get indignant, do I, because I don't understand God's justice? If I am a man, I shouldn't be indignant. Let me go beyond being a man, if I can, and reach the source. But even if I do reach it, I may not tell about it to a human being. Let him go beyond himself also, and reach it with me."[2]

This virtue is also needed in the sciences. Embracing mystery in both theological and scientific equations is not a failure or weakness; it is a level of wise self-awareness and astute observation of the sacred text or natural phenomenon that produces a spiritual maturity we should aim for.

---

2. Allan Fitzgerald, "Naming the Mystery: An Augustinian Ideal," *Religions* 6, no. 1 (March 2015): 204–10, https://doi.org/10.3390/rel6010204.

1 How has my understanding of mystery in theology evolved over my walk with Christ?

• Reflect on how your perception of mystery in your faith has changed over the years. Consider what experiences or teachings have influenced this evolution.

2 In what ways can embracing mystery strengthen my faith and relationship with God?

• Contemplate how accepting the unknown can deepen your relationship with God and enhance your theological insights. Think about the role of humility in this process.

3 How do I balance the pursuit of knowledge with the acceptance of mystery in both my spiritual and scientific inquiries?

• Reflect on how you navigate the desire to understand more about God and the world while acknowledging that some things are beyond human comprehension.

4 What lessons can I learn from historical figures like Isaac Newton and Michael Faraday about integrating faith and scientific discovery?

• Consider how the faith and discoveries of these scientists can inspire your own approach to integrating faith and science. Reflect on how their worldview shaped their contributions to science.

5 How do I interpret the tension between divine

sovereignty and human responsibility as described in John 3:8 and other Scriptures?

• Reflect on how you understand and live with the mystery of God's sovereignty and human culpability. Think about how this tension impacts your faith and actions.

6 IN WHAT WAYS CAN I CULTIVATE A SENSE OF AWE AND wonder in my spiritual and scientific explorations, acknowledging both general and special revelation?

• Reflect on how embracing mystery can lead to a deeper appreciation of God's creation and revelation. Consider practical steps to nurture a sense of wonder in both your faith and scientific studies.

Chapter 4

Conclusion

A Call to Humility

"A paradox is an apparent contradiction. In general the discovery of a paradox is the result of an encounter with a reality which our concepts are inadequate to deal with, a reality that ties us in a conceptual knot. When we try to understand it we find ourselves saying self-contradictory things, but this does not mean that the reality we have encountered is itself self-contradictory. It means that there is a problem with our conceptual equipment."[1]

— Bruce P. Baugus

God called us to be stewards of the Garden of Eden. Our disobedience and subsequent judgment did not negate that command. Thus, we have a responsi-

---

1. Bruce P. Baugus, "Paradox and Mystery in Theology," *The Heythrop Journal* 54, no. 2 (2013): 238–51, https://doi.org/10.1111/j.1468-2265.2011.00735.x.

to move beyond the starting point of God's Word and God's World to actively engage with that world—for good.

Moses' warning in Deuteronomy 29:29 is not solely for theologians but for all believers. It is a call to resist the temptation to complete syllogism without verifiable data—in this case, that data being the inerrant and infallible Word of the living God. Your active participation in this pursuit is crucial. Intellectual limitations are gifts when the only other option is to construct a self-destructive lie.

Both science and theology, in their unique ways, must approach revelation with humility born of limitations. Speculation may not be wrong in a moral sense (in every case) but can be self-delusional if not downright fraudulent. Thus, embracing mystery when variables are unknown and, possibly, unknowable, is a sign of maturity. As we continue our inquiries, let us remember that the most profound truths often lie beyond our immediate grasp, inviting us to explore with humility and wonder.

As Walker Percy once wrote,

> "The search is what anyone would undertake if he were not sunk in the everydayness of his own life. To become aware of the possibility of the search is to be on to something. Not to be on to something is to be in despair."[2]

Indeed, the triumph of mystery is not in its resolution but in its pursuit. And to seek, knock, and inquire (Matthew 7:7-8), with the posture of humility, is, in the revelation of God, the

---

2. Walker Percy. *The Moviegoer*. New York: Random House, 1961, 13.

necessary step to a saving relationship with our Creator (Psalm 25:9; Jeremiah 29:13; Revelation 3:20).[3]

There is no mystery in that.

~

3. "He guides the humble in what is right and teaches them His way" (Psalm 25:9 ESV). "You will seek Me and find Me when you seek Me with all your heart" (Jeremiah 29:13). "Ask, and it will be given to you; seek, and you will find; knock, and it will be opened to you. For everyone who asks receives, and the one who seeks finds, and to the one who knocks it will be opened" (Matthew 7:7-8). "Behold, I stand at the door and knock. If anyone hears My voice and opens the door, I will come in to him and eat with him, and he with Me" (Revelation 3:20).

Questions for Reflection

1 How can I fulfill my role as a steward of God's creation in my daily life?

• Reflect on practical steps you can take to care for the environment and promote the well-being of God's creation. Consider how this stewardship aligns with biblical principles.

2 In what ways can I balance the pursuit of knowledge with the acceptance of mystery in both my spiritual and scientific inquiries?

• Contemplate how you navigate the desire to understand more about God and the world while acknowledging that some things are beyond human comprehension. Reflect on the importance of humility in this balance.

3 How does the warning in Deuteronomy 29:29 influence my approach to understanding and applying Scripture?

• Reflect on how this verse encourages you to resist speculative conclusions and to rely on the revealed truths in God's Word. Consider the implications for your faith and practice.

4 What steps can I take to ensure that my pursuit of knowledge, both scientific and theological, is grounded in humility and reverence for God's revelation?

• Think about ways to cultivate humility in your studies and inquiries. Reflect on how to approach both disciplines with a recognition of your limitations and a respect for divine mystery.

5 How do I respond to Walker Percy's idea that the search for meaning is essential to avoid despair?

• Reflect on how actively seeking knowledge and understanding, both spiritually and scientifically, contributes to a fulfilling and purposeful life. Consider the dangers of complacency and the importance of continuous exploration.

6 In what ways can the scriptural promises of seeking and finding (Matthew 7:7-8; Jeremiah 29:13; Revelation 3:20) guide my approach to both spiritual and intellectual pursuits?

• Contemplate how these promises encourage you to persist in your search for truth and understanding. Reflect on how this persistence impacts your relationship with God and your engagement with the world around you.

Chapter 5

A Prayer

For Transformed Minds

Lord and Father of all, we come to Thee in the name of Thy Son our Savior Jesus Christ and pray that we may increasingly think thoughts after Thee so that by Thy grace and might we may serve Thee with minds and hearts consecrated to Thee and Thy kingdom, more fully doing Your will, O Triune God, in Your world; We pray in the name of our Lord Jesus Christ who lives and reigns with Thee O Father and the Holy Spirit, one God now and forever more. *Amen.*

Chapter 6

Invitation to Receive the Lord Jesus Christ

A Presentation of the Gospel

"Go therefore and make disciples of all the nations, baptizing them in the name of the Father and of the Son and of the Holy Spirit, teaching them to observe all things that I have commanded you; and lo, I am with you always, *even* to the end of the age." Amen.

What is Your Hope of Eternal Life?
Your good works? Religion? Hoping for the best?

The Biblical truth is that:

• Heaven is a free gift; it is neither earned nor deserved (**Ephesians 2:8-9**).

• Man is a sinner and cannot save himself (**Romans 3:23**).

• God is loving but also just. He will judge sin (**Romans 6:23**).

• Since we are sinners and cannot save ourselves, we face a great human crisis. Jesus said unless we turn away from self and sin and trust in Him, we will perish (**Luke 13:3**).

• But God, rich in mercy and grace, sent Jesus Christ, fully God and fully Man, to live the perfect life and pay the penalty for our sins (**Romans 5:8**). He died on the cross for sinners and rose again on the third day (**Romans 10:9**)**,** and seen by over five hundred witnesses who were alive when the Apostles wrote the New Testament (**1 Corinthians 15:6**).

When you repent of your sins and trust in the resurrected Lord Jesus as your Savior, you will be saved (**1 John 1:9**)**.**

If you have not repented and received the Lord Jesus Christ as your Savior, waste no more time and be not presumptuous.

> "For He says:
>> 'In an acceptable time I have heard you,
>> And in the day of salvation I have helped you.'
> Behold, now *is* the accepted time; behold, now *is* the day of salvation" (2 Corinthians 6:2 NKJV).

None of us know the day nor the hour when we shall appear before God. Turn to Jesus Christ right now. The Gospel is that our Lord Jesus lived the life we could not live and died the death that should have been ours. A *Great Exchange* happened on the cross on the hill called Calvary outside of Jerusalem: *When He died on the cross, He took our sins, and we who believe receive His righteousness—a righteousness required to stand before our Creator.*

To receive the Lord Jesus as the resurrected and living Lord of your life, you must turn from your sins, self, and any false hope you might harbor and turn to the Lord Jesus by faith. "For whosoever shall call upon the name of the Lord shall be saved" (Romans 10:13 KJV).

You may call upon Him in prayer, saying:

"Lord, hear me, a sinner, and help me to turn from my sins and transfer my trust from self or any other person or thing to You only. I believe You are the resurrected and reigning Lord of all. Please forgive me and receive me as Your child. Help me to now follow You according to Your Word. In Jesus' name. Amen."

If you have never been baptized, find a Bible-believing community with a pastor set apart (duly ordained) by the Church (**Acts 2:38**). Tell him about your experience of repenting and believing in Christ according to the Scriptures. Any godly Christian shepherd, i.e., a pastor, will help you to confess Christ publicly and be baptized in the community of God's people.

Then, you must follow the Lord through the Bible, prayer, assembling with other believers for growth in grace and knowledge of our Lord Jesus Christ, and telling others what God has done for you.

"And they continued steadfastly in the Apostles' doctrine and fellowship, in the breaking of bread, and in prayers" (Acts 2:42 NKJV).

May God open your mind and heart to believe and to confess Jesus as your resurrected Lord and Savior.

"For God so loved the world, that he gave his only Son, that whoever believes in him should not perish but have eternal life" (**John 3:16**).

~

**LEARN MORE ABOUT THE GOSPEL OF JESUS CHRIST AT
Learn more at https://faithforliving.live/Gospel.**

Bibliography

Baugus, Bruce P. "Paradox and Mystery in Theology." *The Heythrop Journal* 54, no. 2 (2013): 238–51. https://doi.org/10.1111/j.1468-2265.2011.00735.x.

Bavinck, Herman. *Christian Worldview*. Wheaton: Crossway, 2019.

BBC News. "Chile's Stunning Fossil Whale Graveyard Explained." February 26, 2014, sec. Science & Environment. https://www.bbc.com/news/science-environment-26343894.

Beeke, Joel R., and Sinclair B. Ferguson. *Reformed Confessions Harmonized*. Baker Publishing Group, 1999.

David Snoke. "The Apologetic Argument." *The American Scientific Affiliation* 50, no. June (1998): 108–21. https://www.asa3.org/ASA/PSCF/1998/PSCF6-98dyn.html.

Dembski, William A., Casey Luskin, and Joseph M. Holden. *The Comprehensive Guide to Science and Faith: Exploring the Ultimate Questions About Life and the Cosmos*. Eugene, OR: Harvest House Publishers, 2021.

Feldman, Louis H. "Josephus' Portrait of Noah and Its Parallels in Philo, Pseudo-Philo's 'Biblical Antiquities', and Rabbinic Midrashim." *Proceedings of the American Academy for Jewish Research* 55 (1988): 31–57. https://doi.org/10.2307/3622676.

Fitzgerald, Allan. "Naming the Mystery: An Augustinian Ideal." *Religions* 6, no. 1 (March 2015): 204–10. https://doi.org/10.3390/rel6010204.

Frazer, James George. "Ancient Stories of a Great Flood." *The Journal of the Royal Anthropological Institute of Great Britain and Ireland* 46 (1916): 231–83. https://doi.org/10.2307/2843393.

Hagedorn, Eric W. "The Changing Role of Theological Authority in Ockham's Razor." *Res Philosophica* 99, no. 2 (2022): 97–120. https://doi.org/10.11612/resphil.2165.

Hilhorst, A. "The Noah Story: Was It Known to the Greeks?" In *Interpretations of the Flood*, 56–65. Brill, 1999. https://doi.org/10.1163/9789004675605_007.

J. John. "Lessons in Faith from Michael Faraday, the Brilliant Christian Scientist Who Rose from Poverty and Obscurity." *Christian Today*, February 26, 2021. https://www.christiantoday.com/article/lessons.in.faith.from.michael.faraday.the.brilliant.christian.scientist.who.rose.from.poverty.and.obscurity/136432.htm.

Kellner, Alexander W. A. "Fossilized Theropod Soft Tissue." *Nature* 379, no. 6560 (January 1996): 32–32. https://doi.org/10.1038/379032a0.

Kuyper, Abraham. *Common Grace: God's Gifts for a Fallen World, Volume 1*. Bellevue, WA: Lexham Press, 2016.

Lee, James K. *Augustine and the Mystery of the Church*. Fortress Press, 2017.

Mathematical Challenges to Darwin's Theory of Evolution, 2019. https://www.youtube.com/watch?v=noj4phMT9OE.

Meyer, Stephen C. *Darwin's Doubt: The Explosive Origin of Animal Life and the Case for Intelligent Design*. San Francisco: Harper Collins, 2013.

Sarfati, Jonathan D. "D. Russell Humphreys' Cosmology and the 'Timothy Test': A Reply" 11, no. 2 (1997), 195-198.

Schaeffer, Francis A. *How Should We Then Live? (L'Abri 50th Anniversary Edition): The Rise and Decline of Western Thought and Culture*. Wheaton, IL: Crossway, 2005.

Socratic.org. "PEMDAS - Algebra | Socratic." Accessed May 15, 2024. https://socratic.org/algebra/expressions-equations-and-functions/pemdas.

Whale Fossils in the Desert - Evidence for a Worldwide Flood?, 2023. https://www.youtube.com/watch?v=QUV8dEIQYt8.

～

About the Institute

The D. James Kennedy Institute of Reformed Leadership

About the Author

Michael A. Milton, Ph.D. (University of Wales), is a Presbyterian minister (PCA), author, president of Faith for Living, and Senior Fellow at the D. James Kennedy Institute of Reformed Leadership. The former chancellor-president of Reformed Theological Seminary, provost of Erskine Seminary, and Distinguished Professor of Missions and Evangelism, Mike is also a retired Chaplain (Colonel) in the US Army.

He founded and pastored churches in Kansas, Georgia, and North Carolina. He is the former pastor of the historic First Presbyterian Church of Chattanooga.

A graduate of UNC-Chapel Hill, among other associations, Mike resides with his wife Mae in the mountains of Western North Carolina.

Learn more at https://michaelmilton.org/about. He writes

regularly on Substack and for Carolina Journal, Christianity.com, Crosswalk.com, The American Spectator, and other publications.

~

• About Michael A. Milton: https://michaelmilton.org/about
• Michael A. Milton CV: https://michaelmilton.org/cv
• Military Biography: https://michaelmilton.org/military-bio/

Education

PhD (Wales), DMin (Erskine), MPA (UNC-Chapel Hill), MDiv (Knox), BA (MidAmerica Nazarene University), Diploma (now AS) (Defense Language Institute), Post-doctoral certification in Higher Education Teaching and Learning (Bok School, Harvard University)

Credentials

• Board-certified Clinical Pastoral Education
• Board-certified Pastoral Counseling
• Board-certified Chaplain
• Postdoctoral certification in higher education teaching

~

About This Ministry

The D. James Kennedy Institute of Reformed Leadership is a ministry of Faith for Living, Inc., a North Carolina 501(c)(3) Nonprofit Corporation.

Receive weekly Bible audio messages in your inbox: https://faithforliving.live/ffl.

Subscribe to the free newsletter for weekly essays on faithful Christian living in the secular age: https://drmilton.live/home

The following pages are included in our white papers and series to assist those interested in learning more about the faith and vision of our ministry.

DJK Institute

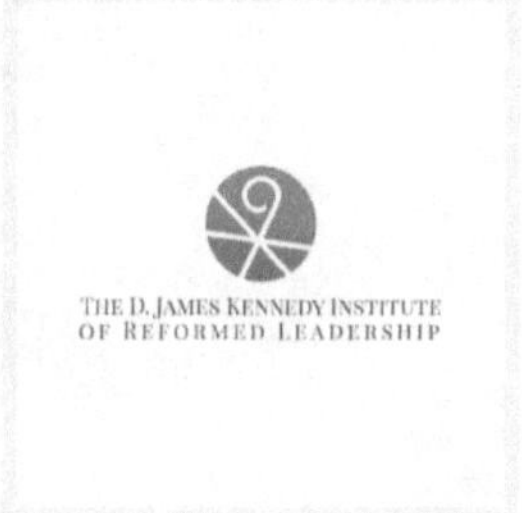

Shepherding shepherds to shepherd the flock

The D. James Kennedy Institute of Reformed Leadership aims to shepherd shepherds to shepherd their flock. This institute is committed to preparing and strengthening leaders with a strong foundation in Reformed theology, using the wisdom of the late Dr. D. James Kennedy. Our goal is to develop servant leaders who exemplify Christ's love and can navigate the complexities of today's world.

~

The D. James Kennedy Institute of Reformed Leadership
The Vision and Mission Statement

First Things

Our Motto: *Excellence in all things and all things for Christ*

Our Anchor Verse: "And you shall know the truth, and the truth shall make you free" (John 8:32).

Our Vision of Teaching:

"The end then of Learning is to repair the ruins of our first Parents by regaining to know God aright, and out of that knowledge to love Him, to imitate Him, to be like Him, as we may the nearest by possessing our souls of true virtue, which being united to the heavenly grace of faith makes up the highest perfection." *On Education* (1644) by John Milton (1608–1674)

Thus, we affirm that a vision and mission statement expresses the identity and work of ministry that progresses from understanding and being captivated by God's Burden,

God's Values, God's Vision, God's Mission, and a God-honoring, Christ-centered Philosophy of Ministry.[1]

Burden: <u>why we exist</u>

The DJK Institute is driven by a burden for the biblical revelation of universal spiritual darkness and its resulting cultural captivity, ensnaring humanity in the devil's domain.

Ephesians 6:12 ESV: "For we do not wrestle against flesh and blood, but against the rulers, against the authorities, against the cosmic powers over this present darkness, against the spiritual forces of evil in the heavenly places."

Values: <u>non-negotiable essentials that guide us</u>

The DJK Institute is grounded in the Holy Scriptures and the Great

Commission and is guided by the principles of the Reformed faith.

Hebrews 4:14 ESV: "Since then we have a great high priest who has passed through the heavens, Jesus, the Son of God, let us hold fast our confession."

Vision: <u>how we lift the burden</u>

Ministering from the transformative light of the Gospel as revealed in the Scriptures, the D. James Kennedy Institute of Reformed Leadership imparts truths that transform, cultivating a faith for living under the sovereign Lordship of Christ.

John 8:31-32 ESV: "So Jesus said to the Jews who had

---

1. Michael A. Milton, Finding a Vision for Your Church: Assembly Required (Phillipsburg, NJ: P & R Publishing, 2012).

believed him, 'If you abide in my word, you are truly my disciples, and you will know the truth, and the truth will set you free.'"

Mission: <u>how we move toward the vision</u>

Our mission is realized through dedicated Research, Writing, and Resource Development in service to the Church.

At the DJK Institute, we:

- Teach transformative truths grounded in John 8:32 and the Reformed and Evangelical faith through engaging biblical truths in public theology.
- Equip and nurture pastoral leaders to shepherd Christ's flock, fostering the development and guidance of fellow shepherds.

Ephesians 6:13 NKJV: "Therefore take up the whole armor of God, that you may be able to withstand in the evil day, and having done all, to stand."

Philosophy of Ministry: <u>how we do our work</u>

In our ministry, we uphold 'Excellence in all things and all things for Christ'—a commitment to God-glorifying excellence. Our teachings, deeply rooted in Scripture and the Reformed faith, aim to foster a 'faith for living' under Christ's Lordship.

Through dedicated research, insightful writing, and comprehensive resources, we support the Cultural Mandate (asserting Christ's Lordship over all life, as per Genesis 1:26-28, 2:15, 9:1), the Great Commandment (loving God and others, as in Matthew 22:35–40, Mark 12:28–34, Luke 10:27a), and the Great Commission (discipling nations, as per Matthew 28:19–20, Acts 1:8).

Matthew 5:16 ESV: "In the same way, let your light shine before others, so that they may see your good works and give glory to your Father who is in heaven."

~

For Those Called to Give

Faith for Living, Inc., is a North Carolina 501(c)(3) Nonprofit Corporation. Inquiries may be directed to info@faithforliving.org. The mailing address is 1167 Carolina Drive, Tryon, NC 28782.

Your gifts sustain the mission of Faith for Living, Inc. Thank you for considering tax-deductible gifts to Faith for Living:

https://michaelmilton.org/give-to-faith-for-living/.

Faith for Living, Inc. is a member of GREAT NONPROFITS. Learn more about our commitment to excellence in nonprofits: https://greatnonprofits.org/org/faith-for-living-inc

~

Acknowledgments

I am forever grateful for the unwavering support of my wife, my son, our children and grandchildren, my dedicated students, the members of the local churches where I had the honor of being your pastor, and my esteemed professors and mentors in the field of Gospel ministry. I must always give thanks to God that He placed me in the care of my Aunt Eva, who taught me the Scriptures from infancy.

It is my sincere hope that this humble essay will assist someone in need. As the author, I have been the recipient of abundant grace from our Lord Jesus Christ and His followers.

Now unto him that is able to do exceeding abundantly above all that we ask or think, according to the power that worketh in us,

Unto him be glory in the church by Christ Jesus throughout all ages, world without end. Amen.

— Saint Paul in the Epistle to the Ephesians 3:20-21